100 WEEKS OF

(THAT'S)

700 DAYS!

MW00961323

Belonging to:

Name ....

Address ....

....

....

Phone ....

Email ....

Weekly Targets:

10	....	60	....
20	....	70	....
30	....	80	....
40	....	90	....
50	....	100	....

If found, kindly return to the contact above.

Thank You!

THE IDEA BEHIND WALKING EVERY DAY

Walking is one of the easiest and most enjoyable ways to find health, lose weight and combat stress.

Simply by putting one foot in front of the other, with a bit of momentum, is all it takes to gain a healthier outlook on life in both body and mind.

Sure, there will be days when we don't feel up to it, such as a rainy day or we're feeling a little under the weather, but the effort will be worth it.

You will find the habit of walking everyday becoming an integral part of your life and will wonder why you haven't become a committed walker before!

This logbook is very simple. Each page has a full week of walking data to fill in. It doesn't matter if you aren't able to walk every day but forming at least a weekly habit is an important part of the journey. Even if you only manage a trip around the block, log it down and record the stats. You will be surprised how quickly the miles add up.

Half a mile or a 10-miler, it doesn't matter just as long as you get out of the house, into the fresh air, and push on.

There is a total of 100 weeks here, or 700 days of walking. If you're doing this to lose weight, only weigh yourself once a week on a designated day and log the results in the columns at the back of the logbook.

If you're doing this to improve your fitness and health, then still fill in the details and see just how lean you can become just by walking every day.

KEEP IT SIMPLE, BUT SAFE

WEAR SUITABLE CLOTHING

Obvious, but important. If you're walking a longer distance than usual, it's almost always best to start with less clothing and layer up if needed.

WEAR COMFORTABLE FOOTWEAR

Absolutely paramount. Painful feet can ruin weeks of future walking, so always try on footwear first and 'break them in' over a couple of short walks. Wear suitable band-aids on toes and heels at first...just in case!

HYDRATE

Carry water on longer walks. Keeping hydrated is especially important when out in the fresh open air. (and don't forget to use sunscreen on those hot days)

1   WEEK START DATE_____

ARGET DISTANCE FOR THIS WEEK [ ]

	Location	Distance Covered	Walking Time Total	Weather Conditions	Feeling? (1-10)
MON					
TUE					
WED					
THU					
FRI					
SAT					
SUN					
TOTALS					

Target Reached?   Yes [ ]   No [ ]

Comments:
....

....

....

....

2   WEEK START DATE _____

TARGET DISTANCE FOR THIS WEEK [   ]

	Location	Distance Covered	Walking Time Total	Weather Conditions	Feeling? (1-10)
MON					
TUE					
WED					
THU					
FRI					
SAT					
SUN					
TOTALS					

Target Reached?   Yes [ ]   No [ ]

Comments:

....

....

....

....

3   WEEK START DATE_____

ARGET DISTANCE FOR THIS WEEK [   ]

	Location	Distance Covered	Walking Time Total	Weather Conditions	Feeling? (1-10)
MON					
TUE					
WED					
THU					
FRI					
SAT					
SUN					
TOTALS					

Target Reached? Yes [ ] No [ ]

mments:

....

....

....

....

4 WEEK START DATE_____

TARGET DISTANCE FOR THIS WEEK [　　]

	Location	Distance Covered	Walking Time Total	Weather Conditions	Feeling? (1-10)
MON					
TUE					
WED					
THU					
FRI					
SAT					
SUN					
TOTALS					

Target Reached? Yes [　] No [　]

Comments:

....

....

....

....

5   WEEK START DATE _____

RGET DISTANCE FOR THIS WEEK ☐

Location	Distance Covered	Walking Time Total	Weather Conditions	Feeling? (1-10)
ON				
UE				
ED				
HU				
RI				
AT				
UN				
TOTALS				

Target Reached?   Yes ☐   No ☐

nments: ....

....

....

....

6   WEEK START DATE_____

TARGET DISTANCE FOR THIS WEEK [　]

	Location	Distance Covered	Walking Time Total	Weather Conditions	Feelin (1-1C
MON					
TUE					
WED					
THU					
FRI					
SAT					
SUN					
TOTALS					

Target Reached?   Yes [　]   No [　]

Comments:

....

....

....

....

7   WEEK START DATE _____

ARGET DISTANCE FOR THIS WEEK ☐

	Location	Distance Covered	Walking Time Total	Weather Conditions	Feeling? (1-10)
MON					
TUE					
WED					
THU					
FRI					
SAT					
SUN					
TOTALS					

Target Reached?   Yes ☐   No ☐

mments: ....

....

....

....

8 WEEK START DATE_____

TARGET DISTANCE FOR THIS WEEK [ ]

	Location	Distance Covered	Walking Time Total	Weather Conditions	Feeling? (1-10)
MON					
TUE					
WED					
THU					
FRI					
SAT					
SUN					
TOTALS					

Target Reached? Yes [ ] No [ ]

Comments:
....

....

....

....

9   WEEK START DATE_____

ARGET DISTANCE FOR THIS WEEK [ ]

	Location	Distance Covered	Walking Time Total	Weather Conditions	Feeling? (1-10)
MON					
TUE					
WED					
THU					
FRI					
SAT					
SUN					
TOTALS					

Target Reached?   Yes [ ]   No [ ]

mments:

....

....

....

....

10 WEEK START DATE_____

TARGET DISTANCE FOR THIS WEEK [   ]

	Location	Distance Covered	Walking Time Total	Weather Conditions	Feeling? (1-10)
MON					
TUE					
WED					
THU					
FRI					
SAT					
SUN					
TOTALS					

Target Reached?   Yes [ ]   No [ ]

Comments:

....

....

....

....

1 WEEK START DATE_____

RGET DISTANCE FOR THIS WEEK ☐

Location	Distance Covered	Walking Time Total	Weather Conditions	Feeling? (1-10)
ON				
UE				
ED				
HU				
RI				
AT				
UN				
TOTALS				

Target Reached? Yes ☐ No ☐

ments:
....

....

....

....

12   WEEK START DATE _____

TARGET DISTANCE FOR THIS WEEK [   ]

	Location	Distance Covered	Walking Time Total	Weather Conditions	Feelin (1-16
MON					
TUE					
WED					
THU					
FRI					
SAT					
SUN					
TOTALS					

Target Reached?   Yes [ ]   No [ ]

Comments:

....

....

....

....

13   WEEK START DATE_____

ARGET DISTANCE FOR THIS WEEK [   ]

	Location	Distance Covered	Walking Time Total	Weather Conditions	Feeling? (1-10)
MON					
TUE					
WED					
THU					
FRI					
SAT					
SUN					
TOTALS					

Target Reached?   Yes [   ]   No [   ]

mments:

....

....

....

....

14 WEEK START DATE_____

TARGET DISTANCE FOR THIS WEEK [   ]

	Location	Distance Covered	Walking Time Total	Weather Conditions	Feeling? (1-10)
MON					
TUE					
WED					
THU					
FRI					
SAT					
SUN					
TOTALS					

Target Reached?   Yes [   ]   No [   ]

Comments:

....

....

....

....

15   WEEK START DATE_____

TARGET DISTANCE FOR THIS WEEK [   ]

Location	Distance Covered	Walking Time Total	Weather Conditions	Feeling? (1-10)
MON				
TUE				
WED				
THU				
FRI				
SAT				
SUN				
TOTALS				

Target Reached?   Yes [   ]   No [   ]

Comments:
....
....
....
....

16 WEEK START DATE_____

TARGET DISTANCE FOR THIS WEEK [ ]

	Location	Distance Covered	Walking Time Total	Weather Conditions	Feeling* (1-10)
MON					
TUE					
WED					
THU					
FRI					
SAT					
SUN					
TOTALS					

Target Reached?   Yes [ ]   No [ ]

Comments:

....

....

....

....

7   WEEK START DATE _____

RGET DISTANCE FOR THIS WEEK ☐

Location	Distance Covered	Walking Time Total	Weather Conditions	Feeling? (1-10)
ON				
UE				
ED				
HU				
RI				
AT				
JN				
TOTALS				

Target Reached?   Yes ☐   No ☐

ıments:

....

....

....

....

18 WEEK START DATE _____

TARGET DISTANCE FOR THIS WEEK [ ]

	Location	Distance Covered	Walking Time Total	Weather Conditions	Feelin (1-10
MON					
TUE					
WED					
THU					
FRI					
SAT					
SUN					
TOTALS					

Target Reached?　Yes [ ]　No [ ]

Comments:

....

....

....

....

19 WEEK START DATE _____

ARGET DISTANCE FOR THIS WEEK [ ]

	Location	Distance Covered	Walking Time Total	Weather Conditions	Feeling? (1-10)
ЛON					
ТUE					
ЛED					
ТHU					
FRI					
ЗАТ					
ЗUN					
TOTALS					

Target Reached?   Yes [ ]   No [ ]

мments: _____

....

....

....

....

20 WEEK START DATE_____

TARGET DISTANCE FOR THIS WEEK [ ]

	Location	Distance Covered	Walking Time Total	Weather Conditions	Feeling? (1-10)
MON					
TUE					
WED					
THU					
FRI					
SAT					
SUN					
TOTALS					

Target Reached?   Yes [ ]   No [ ]

Comments:

....

....

....

....

21 WEEK START DATE _____

ARGET DISTANCE FOR THIS WEEK [   ]

	Location	Distance Covered	Walking Time Total	Weather Conditions	Feeling? (1-10)
MON					
TUE					
WED					
THU					
FRI					
SAT					
SUN					
TOTALS					

Target Reached?   Yes [ ]   No [ ]

Comments:
....

....

....

....

22 WEEK START DATE_____

TARGET DISTANCE FOR THIS WEEK ☐

	Location	Distance Covered	Walking Time Total	Weather Conditions	Feeling (1-10)
MON					
TUE					
WED					
THU					
FRI					
SAT					
SUN					
TOTALS					

Target Reached? Yes ☐ No ☐

Comments:

....

....

....

....

3   WEEK START DATE_____

RGET DISTANCE FOR THIS WEEK [   ]

Location	Distance Covered	Walking Time Total	Weather Conditions	Feeling? (1-10)
ON				
UE				
ED				
HU				
RI				
AT				
JN				
TOTALS				

Target Reached?   Yes [ ]   No [ ]

ıments:
....

....

....

....

24 WEEK START DATE_____

TARGET DISTANCE FOR THIS WEEK [ ]

	Location	Distance Covered	Walking Time Total	Weather Conditions	Feelin (1-1C
MON					
TUE					
WED					
THU					
FRI					
SAT					
SUN					
TOTALS					

Target Reached? Yes [ ] No [ ]

Comments:

....

....

....

....

WEEK START DATE_____

ARGET DISTANCE FOR THIS WEEK

	Location	Distance Covered	Walking Time Total	Weather Conditions	Feeling? (1-10)
MON					
TUE					
WED					
THU					
FRI					
SAT					
SUN					
TOTALS					

Target Reached? Yes ☐ No ☐

mments:

....

....

....

....

26 WEEK START DATE_____

TARGET DISTANCE FOR THIS WEEK ☐

	Location	Distance Covered	Walking Time Total	Weather Conditions	Feeling? (1-10)
MON					
TUE					
WED					
THU					
FRI					
SAT					
SUN					
TOTALS					

Target Reached?   Yes ☐   No ☐

Comments:

....

....

....

....

WEEK START DATE_____

ARGET DISTANCE FOR THIS WEEK [   ]

	Location	Distance Covered	Walking Time Total	Weather Conditions	Feeling? (1-10)
MON					
TUE					
WED					
THU					
FRI					
SAT					
SUN					
TOTALS					

Target Reached? Yes [   ] No [   ]

mments:

....

....

....

....

28 WEEK START DATE_____

TARGET DISTANCE FOR THIS WEEK [　　]

	Location	Distance Covered	Walking Time Total	Weather Conditions	Feeling* (1-10)
MON					
TUE					
WED					
THU					
FRI					
SAT					
SUN					
TOTALS					

Target Reached? Yes [　] No [　]

Comments:

....

....

....

....

WEEK START DATE_____

RGET DISTANCE FOR THIS WEEK ☐

	Location	Distance Covered	Walking Time Total	Weather Conditions	Feeling? (1-10)
ON					
UE					
ED					
HU					
RI					
AT					
UN					
TOTALS					

Target Reached? Yes ☐ No ☐

ments:

....

....

....

....

30 WEEK START DATE_____

TARGET DISTANCE FOR THIS WEEK [   ]

	Location	Distance Covered	Walking Time Total	Weather Conditions	Feeling (1-10
MON					
TUE					
WED					
THU					
FRI					
SAT					
SUN					
TOTALS					

Target Reached? Yes [No [

Comments:

....

....

....

....

31   WEEK START DATE_____

ARGET DISTANCE FOR THIS WEEK [   ]

	Location	Distance Covered	Walking Time Total	Weather Conditions	Feeling? (1-10)
MON					
TUE					
WED					
THU					
FRI					
SAT					
SUN					
TOTALS					

Target Reached?   Yes [   ]   No [   ]

mments:

....

....

....

....

32 WEEK START DATE_____

TARGET DISTANCE FOR THIS WEEK [ ]

	Location	Distance Covered	Walking Time Total	Weather Conditions	Feeling? (1-10)
MON					
TUE					
WED					
THU					
FRI					
SAT					
SUN					
TOTALS					

Target Reached? Yes [ ] No [ ]

Comments:

....

....

....

....

33 WEEK START DATE_____

ARGET DISTANCE FOR THIS WEEK [ ]

	Location	Distance Covered	Walking Time Total	Weather Conditions	Feeling? (1-10)
MON					
TUE					
WED					
THU					
FRI					
SAT					
SUN					
TOTALS					

Target Reached? Yes [ ] No [ ]

mments:
....
....
....
....

34   WEEK START DATE_____

TARGET DISTANCE FOR THIS WEEK ☐

	Location	Distance Covered	Walking Time Total	Weather Conditions	Feeling (1-10)
MON					
TUE					
WED					
THU					
FRI					
SAT					
SUN					
TOTALS					

Target Reached?   Yes ☐   No ☐

Comments:
....

....

....

....

5 WEEK START DATE_____

RGET DISTANCE FOR THIS WEEK ☐

	Location	Distance Covered	Walking Time Total	Weather Conditions	Feeling? (1-10)
ON					
UE					
ED					
HU					
RI					
AT					
JN					
TOTALS					

Target Reached? Yes ☐ No ☐

ments:

....

....

....

....

36 WEEK START DATE _____

TARGET DISTANCE FOR THIS WEEK [ ]

	Location	Distance Covered	Walking Time Total	Weather Conditions	Feelin (1-10
MON					
TUE					
WED					
THU					
FRI					
SAT					
SUN					
TOTALS					

Target Reached? Yes [ ] No [ ]

Comments:

....

....

....

....

37 WEEK START DATE _____

ARGET DISTANCE FOR THIS WEEK ☐

	Location	Distance Covered	Walking Time Total	Weather Conditions	Feeling? (1-10)
MON					
TUE					
WED					
THU					
FRI					
SAT					
SUN					
TOTALS					

Target Reached? Yes ☐ No ☐

mments:

....

....

....

....

38 WEEK START DATE_____

TARGET DISTANCE FOR THIS WEEK [   ]

	Location	Distance Covered	Walking Time Total	Weather Conditions	Feeling (1-10)
MON					
TUE					
WED					
THU					
FRI					
SAT					
SUN					
TOTALS					

Target Reached?   Yes [ ]   No [ ]

Comments:

....

....

....

....

39 WEEK START DATE _____

ARGET DISTANCE FOR THIS WEEK [ ]

	Location	Distance Covered	Walking Time Total	Weather Conditions	Feeling? (1-10)
MON					
TUE					
WED					
THU					
FRI					
SAT					
SUN					
TOTALS					

Target Reached? Yes [ ] No [ ]

mments:

....

....

....

....

40 WEEK START DATE_____

TARGET DISTANCE FOR THIS WEEK [ ]

	Location	Distance Covered	Walking Time Total	Weather Conditions	Feeling (1-10)
MON					
TUE					
WED					
THU					
FRI					
SAT					
SUN					
TOTALS					

Target Reached? Yes [ ] No [ ]

Comments:

....

....

....

....

1   WEEK START DATE_____

RGET DISTANCE FOR THIS WEEK

Location	Distance Covered	Walking Time Total	Weather Conditions	Feeling? (1-10)
ON				
UE				
ED				
HU				
RI				
AT				
JN				
TOTALS				

Target Reached?   Yes ☐   No ☐

ıments:

....

....

....

....

42 WEEK START DATE_____

TARGET DISTANCE FOR THIS WEEK

	Location	Distance Covered	Walking Time Total	Weather Conditions	Feeling (1-10
MON					
TUE					
WED					
THU					
FRI					
SAT					
SUN					
TOTALS					

Target Reached? Yes ☐ No ☐

Comments:

....

....

....

....

ARGET DISTANCE FOR THIS WEEK ☐

	Location	Distance Covered	Walking Time Total	Weather Conditions	Feeling? (1-10)
MON					
TUE					
WED					
THU					
FRI					
SAT					
SUN					
TOTALS					

Target Reached?   Yes ☐   No ☐

mments:

....

....

....

....

44 WEEK START DATE_____

TARGET DISTANCE FOR THIS WEEK [ ]

	Location	Distance Covered	Walking Time Total	Weather Conditions	Feeling? (1-10)
MON					
TUE					
WED					
THU					
FRI					
SAT					
SUN					
TOTALS					

Target Reached? Yes [ ] No [ ]

Comments:
....

....

....

45   WEEK START DATE _____

ARGET DISTANCE FOR THIS WEEK [   ]

	Location	Distance Covered	Walking Time Total	Weather Conditions	Feeling? (1-10)
MON					
TUE					
WED					
THU					
FRI					
SAT					
SUN					
TOTALS					

Target Reached?   Yes [ ]   No [ ]

mments:

....

....

....

....

46 WEEK START DATE_____

TARGET DISTANCE FOR THIS WEEK [ ]

	Location	Distance Covered	Walking Time Total	Weather Conditions	Feeling* (1-10)
MON					
TUE					
WED					
THU					
FRI					
SAT					
SUN					
TOTALS					

Target Reached? Yes [ ] No [ ]

Comments:

....

....

....

....

RGET DISTANCE FOR THIS WEEK [   ]

Location	Distance Covered	Walking Time Total	Weather Conditions	Feeling? (1-10)
ON				
UE				
ED				
HU				
RI				
AT				
JN				
TOTALS				

Target Reached?   Yes [   ]   No [   ]

ments:

....

....

....

....

48 WEEK START DATE_____

TARGET DISTANCE FOR THIS WEEK [____]

	Location	Distance Covered	Walking Time Total	Weather Conditions	Feelin (1-10
MON					
TUE					
WED					
THU					
FRI					
SAT					
SUN					
TOTALS					

Target Reached?   Yes [ ]   No [ ]

Comments:

....

....

....

....

49 WEEK START DATE_____

TARGET DISTANCE FOR THIS WEEK [   ]

	Location	Distance Covered	Walking Time Total	Weather Conditions	Feeling? (1-10)
MON					
TUE					
WED					
THU					
FRI					
SAT					
SUN					
TOTALS					

Target Reached?   Yes [   ]   No [   ]

Comments:
....

....

....

....

50 WEEK START DATE_____

TARGET DISTANCE FOR THIS WEEK ▢

	Location	Distance Covered	Walking Time Total	Weather Conditions	Feeling? (1-10)
MON					
TUE					
WED					
THU					
FRI					
SAT					
SUN					
TOTALS					

Target Reached?   Yes ▢   No ▢

Comments:

....

....

....

....

51 WEEK START DATE _____

TARGET DISTANCE FOR THIS WEEK [ ]

	Location	Distance Covered	Walking Time Total	Weather Conditions	Feeling? (1-10)
MON					
TUE					
WED					
THU					
FRI					
SAT					
SUN					
TOTALS					

Target Reached?　Yes [ ]　No [ ]

Comments:

....

....

....

....

52   WEEK START DATE_____

TARGET DISTANCE FOR THIS WEEK [   ]

	Location	Distance Covered	Walking Time Total	Weather Conditions	Feeling (1-10)
MON					
TUE					
WED					
THU					
FRI					
SAT					
SUN					
TOTALS					

Target Reached?   Yes [ ]   No [ ]

Comments:

....

....

....

....

3 WEEK START DATE_____

RGET DISTANCE FOR THIS WEEK [ ]

Location	Distance Covered	Walking Time Total	Weather Conditions	Feeling? (1-10)
ON				
UE				
ED				
HU				
RI				
AT				
JN				
TOTALS				

Target Reached?   Yes [ ]   No [ ]

nments:

....

....

....

....

54 WEEK START DATE_____

TARGET DISTANCE FOR THIS WEEK [ ]

	Location	Distance Covered	Walking Time Total	Weather Conditions	Feelin (1-10
MON					
TUE					
WED					
THU					
FRI					
SAT					
SUN					
TOTALS					

Target Reached? Yes [ ] No [ ]

Comments:

....

....

....

....

55 WEEK START DATE_____

ARGET DISTANCE FOR THIS WEEK [   ]

	Location	Distance Covered	Walking Time Total	Weather Conditions	Feeling? (1-10)
MON					
TUE					
WED					
THU					
FRI					
SAT					
SUN					
TOTALS					

Target Reached? Yes [   ] No [   ]

mments:

....

....

....

....

56 WEEK START DATE_____

TARGET DISTANCE FOR THIS WEEK [ ]

	Location	Distance Covered	Walking Time Total	Weather Conditions	Feeling? (1-10)
MON					
TUE					
WED					
THU					
FRI					
SAT					
SUN					
TOTALS					

Target Reached? Yes [ ] No [ ]

Comments:
....
....
....
....

WEEK START DATE_____

ARGET DISTANCE FOR THIS WEEK [   ]

	Location	Distance Covered	Walking Time Total	Weather Conditions	Feeling? (1-10)
MON					
TUE					
WED					
THU					
FRI					
SAT					
SUN					
TOTALS					

Target Reached? Yes [   ] No [   ]

Comments:

....

....

....

....

58 WEEK START DATE_____

TARGET DISTANCE FOR THIS WEEK [ ]

	Location	Distance Covered	Walking Time Total	Weather Conditions	Feeling (1-10)
MON					
TUE					
WED					
THU					
FRI					
SAT					
SUN					
TOTALS					

Target Reached? Yes [ ] No [ ]

Comments:

....

....

....

....

WEEK START DATE_____

RGET DISTANCE FOR THIS WEEK

	Location	Distance Covered	Walking Time Total	Weather Conditions	Feeling? (1-10)
ON					
UE					
ED					
HU					
RI					
AT					
JN					
TOTALS					

Target Reached? Yes ☐ No ☐

ments:

....

....

....

....

60 WEEK START DATE_____

TARGET DISTANCE FOR THIS WEEK [ ]

	Location	Distance Covered	Walking Time Total	Weather Conditions	Feeling (1-10
MON					
TUE					
WED					
THU					
FRI					
SAT					
SUN					
TOTALS					

Target Reached?   Yes [ ]   No [ ]

Comments:

....

....

....

....

61 WEEK START DATE_____

ARGET DISTANCE FOR THIS WEEK [ ]

	Location	Distance Covered	Walking Time Total	Weather Conditions	Feeling? (1-10)
MON					
TUE					
WED					
THU					
FRI					
SAT					
SUN					
TOTALS					

Target Reached? Yes [ ] No [ ]

mments:

....

....

....

....

62 WEEK START DATE_____

TARGET DISTANCE FOR THIS WEEK

	Location	Distance Covered	Walking Time Total	Weather Conditions	Feeling? (1-10)
MON					
TUE					
WED					
THU					
FRI					
SAT					
SUN					
TOTALS					

Target Reached? Yes ☐ No ☐

Comments:

....

....

....

....

63 WEEK START DATE_____

ARGET DISTANCE FOR THIS WEEK ☐

	Location	Distance Covered	Walking Time Total	Weather Conditions	Feeling? (1-10)
MON					
TUE					
WED					
THU					
FRI					
SAT					
SUN					
TOTALS					

Target Reached? Yes ☐ No ☐

mments:

....

....

....

....

64 WEEK START DATE_____

TARGET DISTANCE FOR THIS WEEK [ ]

	Location	Distance Covered	Walking Time Total	Weather Conditions	Feeling? (1-10)
MON					
TUE					
WED					
THU					
FRI					
SAT					
SUN					
TOTALS					

Target Reached? Yes [ ] No [ ]

Comments:
....

....

....

....

5   WEEK START DATE_____

RGET DISTANCE FOR THIS WEEK [ ]

Location	Distance Covered	Walking Time Total	Weather Conditions	Feeling? (1-10)
ON				
UE				
ED				
HU				
RI				
AT				
UN				
TOTALS				

Target Reached?   Yes [ ]   No [ ]

nments:

....

....

....

....

66 WEEK START DATE_____

TARGET DISTANCE FOR THIS WEEK [ ]

	Location	Distance Covered	Walking Time Total	Weather Conditions	Feelin (1-10
MON					
TUE					
WED					
THU					
FRI					
SAT					
SUN					
TOTALS					

Target Reached? Yes [ ] No [ ]

Comments:

....

....

....

....

....

WEEK START DATE_____

ARGET DISTANCE FOR THIS WEEK [   ]

	Location	Distance Covered	Walking Time Total	Weather Conditions	Feeling? (1-10)
MON					
TUE					
WED					
THU					
FRI					
SAT					
SUN					
TOTALS					

Target Reached? Yes [   ] No [   ]

Comments:

....

....

....

....

68 WEEK START DATE_____

TARGET DISTANCE FOR THIS WEEK

	Location	Distance Covered	Walking Time Total	Weather Conditions	Feeling? (1-10)
MON					
TUE					
WED					
THU					
FRI					
SAT					
SUN					
TOTALS					

Target Reached? Yes ☐ No ☐

Comments:

....

....

....

....

WEEK START DATE_____

ARGET DISTANCE FOR THIS WEEK ☐

	Location	Distance Covered	Walking Time Total	Weather Conditions	Feeling? (1-10)
MON					
TUE					
WED					
THU					
FRI					
SAT					
SUN					
TOTALS					

Target Reached? Yes ☐ No ☐

mments:

....

....

....

....

70 WEEK START DATE_____

TARGET DISTANCE FOR THIS WEEK [   ]

	Location	Distance Covered	Walking Time Total	Weather Conditions	Feeling (1-10)
MON					
TUE					
WED					
THU					
FRI					
SAT					
SUN					
TOTALS					

Target Reached? Yes [   ] No [   ]

Comments:

....

....

....

....

1 WEEK START DATE_____

RGET DISTANCE FOR THIS WEEK [   ]

Location	Distance Covered	Walking Time Total	Weather Conditions	Feeling? (1-10)
ON				
UE				
ED				
HU				
RI				
AT				
UN				
TOTALS				

Target Reached? Yes [ ] No [ ]

ments:

....

....

....

....

72 WEEK START DATE_____

TARGET DISTANCE FOR THIS WEEK [　]

	Location	Distance Covered	Walking Time Total	Weather Conditions	Feelin (1-1C
MON					
TUE					
WED					
THU					
FRI					
SAT					
SUN					
TOTALS					

Target Reached? Yes [　] No [　]

Comments:

....

....

....

....

73 WEEK START DATE_____

ARGET DISTANCE FOR THIS WEEK [ ]

Location	Distance Covered	Walking Time Total	Weather Conditions	Feeling? (1-10)
MON				
TUE				
WED				
THU				
FRI				
SAT				
SUN				
TOTALS				

Target Reached?   Yes [ ]   No [ ]

mments:
....
....
....
....

74   WEEK START DATE _____

TARGET DISTANCE FOR THIS WEEK [   ]

	Location	Distance Covered	Walking Time Total	Weather Conditions	Feeling? (1-10)
MON					
TUE					
WED					
THU					
FRI					
SAT					
SUN					
TOTALS					

Target Reached?   Yes [ ]   No [ ]

Comments:

....

....

....

....

75 WEEK START DATE_____

TARGET DISTANCE FOR THIS WEEK [　　]

	Location	Distance Covered	Walking Time Total	Weather Conditions	Feeling? (1-10)
MON					
TUE					
WED					
THU					
FRI					
SAT					
SUN					
TOTALS					

Target Reached?   Yes [　]   No [　]

Comments:

....

....

....

....

76 WEEK START DATE_____

TARGET DISTANCE FOR THIS WEEK [　　]

	Location	Distance Covered	Walking Time Total	Weather Conditions	Feeling (1-10)
MON					
TUE					
WED					
THU					
FRI					
SAT					
SUN					
TOTALS					

Target Reached? Yes [　] No [　]

Comments:

....

....

....

....

7 WEEK START DATE_____

RGET DISTANCE FOR THIS WEEK ⬜

Location	Distance Covered	Walking Time Total	Weather Conditions	Feeling? (1-10)
ON				
UE				
ED				
HU				
RI				
AT				
JN				
TOTALS				

Target Reached? Yes ⬜ No ⬜

ments:

....

....

....

....

78   WEEK START DATE_____

TARGET DISTANCE FOR THIS WEEK [   ]

	Location	Distance Covered	Walking Time Total	Weather Conditions	Feeling (1-10
MON					
TUE					
WED					
THU					
FRI					
SAT					
SUN					
TOTALS					

Target Reached?   Yes [ ]   No [ ]

Comments:

....

....

....

....

79 WEEK START DATE_____

ARGET DISTANCE FOR THIS WEEK [   ]

	Location	Distance Covered	Walking Time Total	Weather Conditions	Feeling? (1-10)
MON					
TUE					
WED					
THU					
FRI					
SAT					
SUN					
TOTALS					

Target Reached? Yes [ ] No [ ]

mments:

....

....

....

....

80 WEEK START DATE_____

TARGET DISTANCE FOR THIS WEEK [   ]

	Location	Distance Covered	Walking Time Total	Weather Conditions	Feeling? (1-10)
MON					
TUE					
WED					
THU					
FRI					
SAT					
SUN					
TOTALS					

Target Reached?   Yes [ ]   No [ ]

Comments:

....

....

....

....

81 WEEK START DATE_____

ARGET DISTANCE FOR THIS WEEK [   ]

Location	Distance Covered	Walking Time Total	Weather Conditions	Feeling? (1-10)
MON				
TUE				
WED				
THU				
FRI				
SAT				
SUN				
TOTALS				

Target Reached?   Yes [   ]   No [   ]

mments:

....

....

....

....

82   WEEK START DATE _____

TARGET DISTANCE FOR THIS WEEK [   ]

	Location	Distance Covered	Walking Time Total	Weather Conditions	Feeling (1-10)
MON					
TUE					
WED					
THU					
FRI					
SAT					
SUN					
TOTALS					

Target Reached?   Yes [ ]   No [ ]

Comments:

....

....

....

....

3 WEEK START DATE _____

RGET DISTANCE FOR THIS WEEK [   ]

Location	Distance Covered	Walking Time Total	Weather Conditions	Feeling? (1-10)
ON				
UE				
ED				
HU				
RI				
AT				
JN				
TOTALS				

Target Reached? Yes [   ] No [   ]

ments:

....

....

....

....

84   WEEK START DATE_____

TARGET DISTANCE FOR THIS WEEK [   ]

	Location	Distance Covered	Walking Time Total	Weather Conditions	Feelin (1-1C
MON					
TUE					
WED					
THU					
FRI					
SAT					
SUN					
TOTALS					

Target Reached?   Yes [   ]   No [   ]

Comments:

....

....

....

....

85 WEEK START DATE_____

TARGET DISTANCE FOR THIS WEEK [   ]

	Location	Distance Covered	Walking Time Total	Weather Conditions	Feeling? (1-10)
MON					
TUE					
WED					
THU					
FRI					
SAT					
SUN					
TOTALS					

Target Reached?   Yes [   ]   No [   ]

Comments:

....

....

....

....

86 WEEK START DATE _____

TARGET DISTANCE FOR THIS WEEK [   ]

	Location	Distance Covered	Walking Time Total	Weather Conditions	Feeling? (1-10)
MON					
TUE					
WED					
THU					
FRI					
SAT					
SUN					
TOTALS					

Target Reached? Yes [   ] No [   ]

Comments:

....

....

....

....

WEEK START DATE_____

ARGET DISTANCE FOR THIS WEEK

Location	Distance Covered	Walking Time Total	Weather Conditions	Feeling? (1-10)
MON				
TUE				
WED				
THU				
FRI				
SAT				
SUN				
TOTALS				

Target Reached?   Yes ☐   No ☐

Comments:

....

....

....

....

88   WEEK START DATE _____

TARGET DISTANCE FOR THIS WEEK [   ]

	Location	Distance Covered	Walking Time Total	Weather Conditions	Feeling* (1-10)
MON					
TUE					
WED					
THU					
FRI					
SAT					
SUN					
TOTALS					

Target Reached?   Yes [ ]   No [ ]

Comments:

....

....

....

....

9 WEEK START DATE_____

RGET DISTANCE FOR THIS WEEK ☐

Location	Distance Covered	Walking Time Total	Weather Conditions	Feeling? (1-10)
ON				
UE				
ED				
HU				
RI				
AT				
JN				
TOTALS				

Target Reached?   Yes ☐   No ☐

ments:

....

....

....

....

90 WEEK START DATE_____

TARGET DISTANCE FOR THIS WEEK ☐

	Location	Distance Covered	Walking Time Total	Weather Conditions	Feeling (1-10
MON					
TUE					
WED					
THU					
FRI					
SAT					
SUN					
TOTALS					

Target Reached? Yes ☐ No ☐

Comments:

....

....

....

....

91   WEEK START DATE_____

ARGET DISTANCE FOR THIS WEEK [ ]

	Location	Distance Covered	Walking Time Total	Weather Conditions	Feeling? (1-10)
MON					
TUE					
WED					
THU					
FRI					
SAT					
SUN					
TOTALS					

Target Reached?   Yes [ ]   No [ ]

mments:

....

....

....

....

92   WEEK START DATE_____

TARGET DISTANCE FOR THIS WEEK [ ]

	Location	Distance Covered	Walking Time Total	Weather Conditions	Feeling? (1-10)
MON					
TUE					
WED					
THU					
FRI					
SAT					
SUN					
TOTALS					

Target Reached?   Yes [ ]   No [ ]

Comments:

....

....

....

....

WEEK START DATE_____

ARGET DISTANCE FOR THIS WEEK ☐

	Location	Distance Covered	Walking Time Total	Weather Conditions	Feeling? (1-10)
MON					
TUE					
WED					
THU					
FRI					
SAT					
SUN					
TOTALS					

Target Reached?   Yes ☐   No ☐

mments:

....

....

....

....

94 WEEK START DATE_____

TARGET DISTANCE FOR THIS WEEK [ ]

	Location	Distance Covered	Walking Time Total	Weather Conditions	Feeling (1-10)
MON					
TUE					
WED					
THU					
FRI					
SAT					
SUN					
TOTALS					

Target Reached? Yes [ ] No [ ]

Comments:
....
....
....
....

5   WEEK START DATE_____

RGET DISTANCE FOR THIS WEEK [   ]

Location	Distance Covered	Walking Time Total	Weather Conditions	Feeling? (1-10)
ON				
UE				
ED				
HU				
RI				
AT				
UN				
TOTALS				

Target Reached?   Yes [   ]   No [   ]

nments:
....

....

....

....

96 WEEK START DATE_____

TARGET DISTANCE FOR THIS WEEK [ ]

	Location	Distance Covered	Walking Time Total	Weather Conditions	Feelin (1-1C
MON					
TUE					
WED					
THU					
FRI					
SAT					
SUN					
TOTALS					

Target Reached?   Yes [ ]   No [ ]

Comments:

....

....

....

....

97 WEEK START DATE_____

ARGET DISTANCE FOR THIS WEEK [ ]

	Location	Distance Covered	Walking Time Total	Weather Conditions	Feeling? (1-10)
MON					
TUE					
WED					
THU					
FRI					
SAT					
SUN					
TOTALS					

Target Reached? Yes [ ] No [ ]

mments:

....

....

....

....

98   WEEK START DATE_____

TARGET DISTANCE FOR THIS WEEK [   ]

	Location	Distance Covered	Walking Time Total	Weather Conditions	Feeling? (1-10)
MON					
TUE					
WED					
THU					
FRI					
SAT					
SUN					
TOTALS					

Target Reached?   Yes [   ]   No [   ]

Comments:

....

....

....

....

99 WEEK START DATE_____

ARGET DISTANCE FOR THIS WEEK [   ]

	Location	Distance Covered	Walking Time Total	Weather Conditions	Feeling? (1-10)
MON					
TUE					
WED					
THU					
FRI					
SAT					
SUN					
TOTALS					

Target Reached? Yes [   ] No [   ]

mments:

....

....

....

....

100 WEEK START DATE_____

TARGET DISTANCE FOR THIS WEEK [   ]

	Location	Distance Covered	Walking Time Total	Weather Conditions	Feeling (1-10)
MON					
TUE					
WED					
THU					
FRI					
SAT					
SUN					
TOTALS					

Target Reached? Yes [ ] No [ ]

Comments:

....

....

....

....

AT-A-GLANCE &
STAT RECORDS

AT-A-GLANCE WALKING RECORDS

Week	Start Date	Distance	Total Time	Steps	Feeling 1
1					
2					
3					
4					
5					
6					
7					
8					
9					
10					
11					
12					
13					
14					
15					
16					
17					
18					
19					
20					
21					
22					
23					
24					
25					
Page Walk Total					

AT-A-GLANCE WALKING RECORDS

Week	Start Date	Distance	Total Time	Steps	Feeling 1-10
26					
27					
28					
29					
30					
31					
32					
33					
34					
35					
36					
37					
38					
39					
40					
41					
42					
43					
44					
45					
46					
47					
48					
49					
50					
Page Walk Total					

AT-A-GLANCE WALKING RECORDS

Week	Start Date	Distance	Total Time	Steps	Feeling 1-1
51					
52					
53					
54					
55					
56					
57					
58					
59					
60					
61					
62					
63					
64					
65					
66					
67					
68					
69					
70					
71					
72					
73					
74					
75					
Page Walk Total					

AT-A-GLANCE WALKING RECORDS

Week	Start Date	Distance	Total Time	Steps	Feeling 1-10
76					
77					
78					
79					
80					
81					
82					
83					
84					
85					
86					
87					
88					
89					
90					
91					
92					
93					
94					
95					
96					
97					
98					
99					
100					
Page Walk Total					

WEIGHT STATS – TARGET IN LBS @ 25 WEEKS

Week	Start Weight	'Now' Weight	Lost	Gained	Total for wk.	Total Lo
1						
2						
3						
4						
5						
6						
7						
8						
9						
10						
11						
12						
13						
14						
15						
16						
17						
18						
19						
20						
21						
22						
23						
24						
25						

25 Week Total

EIGHT STATS – TARGET IN LBS @ 50 WEEKS

ek	Start Weight	'Now' Weight	Lost	Gained	Total for wk.	Total Lost
6						
7						
8						
9						
0						
1						
2						
3						
4						
5						
6						
7						
8						
9						
0						
1						
2						
3						
4						
5						
6						
7						
8						
9						
0						
					50 Walk Total	

WEIGHT STATS – TARGET IN LBS @ 75 WEEKS

Week	Start Weight	'Now' Weight	Lost	Gained	Total for wk.	Total L
51						
52						
53						
54						
55						
56						
57						
58						
59						
60						
61						
62						
63						
64						
65						
66						
67						
68						
69						
70						
71						
72						
73						
74						
75						

75 Week Total

WEIGHT STATS – TARGET IN LBS @ 100 WEEKS

Week	Start Weight	'Now' Weight	Lost	Gained	Total for wk.	Total Lost
76						
77						
78						
79						
80						
81						
82						
83						
84						
85						
86						
87						
88						
89						
90						
91						
92						
93						
94						
95						
96						
97						
98						
99						
00						

100 Walk Total

After 700 walks, there must be one that stands out and one you would rather leave behind. Jot them down here for the memories as well as your longest and 'most time taken' walks.

	WEEK NO.	DATE	RATING
LONGEST WALK BY DISTANCE			
LONGEST WALK BY TIME			
MOST ENJOYED WALK			
WORST WALK			

If you have completed all 700 walks, you must have gone through plenty of footwear. Some excellent, some OK, and some that nearly crippled you. Keep a record, ongoing, here to remember the good, the bad and the ugly!

BRAND	ACQUIRED	COMMENT

As well as going through an array of footwear, what other items of clothing impressed or disappointed you? Log them here for future reference.

CLOTHING BRAND & TYPE	ACQUIRED	COMMENT

Made in the USA
Las Vegas, NV
28 March 2024

87930289R00066